NANA,

I WROTE THIS BOOK ABOUT YOU

IT'S ME

ABOUT THE AUTHOR!

My name is .... I am .... years old.

I wrote this book about you because

....

....

....

MY NANA

ABOUT MY NANA!

My Nana's name is .... She is ....

years old. Her hair is .... Her favorite food

is .... and she loves to watch ....

.... She looks like ....

Her best feature is ....

My Nana is special because

MY AWESOME NANA!

My Nana is .... at so many things.

But she is the best at ....

....

I admire my Nana because

Three words I would use to describe my Nana.

HERE IS A PICTURE

I'm thankful for
my Nana because

My favorite thing about Nana is

....

....

....

....

Draw a picture

MY INCREDIBLE NANA!

My Nana is my ....

When I grow up, I want to be as ....

and .... as my Nana!

My Nana makes me laugh when

....

....

....

....

When I need help with

....

....

....

....

.... I ask my Nana.

People that know my Nana says she

....

....

....

....

....

MY AMAZING NANA!

My Nana is the .... Nana. She is funny

when she .... She always makes

me .... I love it when Nana ....

....

My Nana and I like to

I love it when she

DRAW A PICTURE

MY SUPERHERO NANA!

My Nana's superhero name is ....

....

Her superpower is ....

....

MY SUPER NANA

When I feel sick, she

We always play

Nana likes to say

If I could go anywhere in the world with my Nana,

We would go to ....

....

....

My favorite memory of my Nana

ME AND NANA!

I LOVE MY NANA!

My Nana is stronger than ....

cooler than ....

and more smart than ....

....

My Nana is proud of me when

My Nana likes to eat ....

She likes to drink ....

and also she cooks the yummiest ....

....

I'm so happy when my Nana

....

....

....

....

My Nana taught me how to

MY FAVORITE PICTURE OF NANA!

My Nana is always there for me when

I feel safe when you

....

....

....

....

....

Thank you for being patient with me when

MY NANA

You will always be my ....

....

....

....

....

On this special day, I want my Nana to know

FAMILY PICTURE!

I LOVE YOU NANA!

Nana, I wrote a poem for you

THANK YOU FOR BEING AN AWESOME NANA!

Made in the USA
Coppell, TX
19 May 2025

49510640R00024